T0071139

Will Todd

Passion Music

for female gospel soloist,
SATB, and jazz ensemble

MUSIC DEPARTMENT

OXFORD
UNIVERSITY PRESS

OXFORD
UNIVERSITY PRESS

Great Clarendon Street, Oxford OX2 6DP,
United Kingdom

Oxford University Press is a department of the University of Oxford.
It furthers the University's aim of excellence in research, scholarship,
and education by publishing worldwide. Oxford is a registered trade mark of
Oxford University Press in the UK and in certain other countries

© Oxford University Press 2018

Will Todd has asserted his right under the Copyright, Designs
and Patents Act, 1988, to be identified as the Composer of this Work

First published 2018

All rights reserved. No part of this publication may be reproduced,
stored in a retrieval system, or transmitted, in any form or by any means,
without the prior permission in writing of Oxford University Press,
or as expressly permitted by law.

Permission to perform this work in public (except in the course of divine worship)
should normally be obtained from a local performing right licensing organization,
unless the owner or the occupier of the premises being used already holds a licence
from such an organization. Likewise, permission to make and exploit a recording of this work
should be obtained from a local mechanical copyright licensing organization

Enquiries concerning reproduction outside the scope of the above
should be directed to the Music Rights Department, Oxford University Press,
at music.permissions.uk@oup.com or at the address above

ISBN 978-0-19-352380-7

Music and text origination by
Andrew Jones

Printed in Great Britain on acid-free paper by
Halstan & Co. Ltd, Amersham, Bucks.

Contents

1. Greater Love 1
2. We Believe 13
3. A New Commandment 24
4. Love Unknown 38
5. Stabat Mater 49
6. The Seven Last Words from the Cross 57
7. My Love has Died for Me 76
8. Do not stand at my grave and weep 81
9. Were you there? 92

Composer's note

Since composing *Mass in Blue* in 2003 I have been searching for another large-scale project in which to showcase my love of jazz improvising and the beauty and energy of the choral sound. Finally, in 2017, an opportunity arose to create a new jazz choral work for the choirs of St Martin-in-the-Fields, and *Passion Music* is the product of that. The work is an exploration of Easter-themed texts, roughly following the contours of the passion narrative, and uses a soloist as an inspirational and evangelistic voice leading the emotional direction of the complete piece, rather than in the traditional sense of narrating the gospel text. I was thrilled to be able to work with Shaneeka Simon in developing a truly gospel solo part to weave in and around the ensemble and choral textures.

Passion Music has nine movements, mixing hymn texts, gospel quotations, and texts of my own. The rhythm section music, although fully notated, will benefit from improvising performers, who are encouraged to bring their own ideas and textures to the work, making use of the chord symbols. It is also expected that the solo part will be embellished in performance, and there are free improvising sections indicated by wavy lines and appropriate chord symbols. Not all the notated ornamentation needs to be followed—the soloist should feel free to find their own authentic gospel style. Note that the keyboard reduction in the vocal score is for rehearsal only, and the full ensemble backing is required for performance. Pedalling in the keyboard part is marked when specific effects are required; otherwise the player should use the pedal *ad lib.* throughout. *Passion Music* may also be performed liturgically with interspersed readings.

Duration: *c.*40 mins

This note may be reproduced as required for programme notes.

Passion Music was first performed by the choirs of St Martin-in-the-Fields and The Will Todd Ensemble, with Shaneeka Simon, directed by the composer, on 27 March 2018 at St Martin-in-the-Fields, London.

Texts and translations

These texts may be reproduced as required for programme notes.

1. Greater Love

John 15: 13

Greater love has no man, no greater love than this, than to lay down his life for his friends.

2. We Believe

Mrs Cecil Frances Alexander (1818–95)

There is a green hill far away,
Without a city wall,
Where the dear Lord was crucified,
Who died to save us all.

We may not know, we cannot tell,
What pains he had to bear,
But we believe it was for us
He hung and suffered there.

He died that we might be forgiven,
He died to make us good,
That we might go at last to heaven,
Saved by his precious blood.

There was no other good enough
To pay the price of sin;
For only he could unlock the gate
Of heaven and let us in.

3. A New Commandment

John 13: 34

I give you a new commandment:
That you love one another as I have loved you.

4. Love Unknown

Samuel Crossman (1624–84)

My song is love unknown,
My saviour's love to me;
Love to the loveless shown,
That they might lovely be.
O who am I, that for my sake
My Lord should take frail flesh and die?

He came from his blest throne,
Salvation to bestow;
But men made strange,
And none the longed-for Christ would know.
But O, my friend, my friend indeed,
Who at my need his life did spend.

Sometimes they strew his way
And his sweet praises sing;
Resounding all the day
Hosannas to their King.
Then 'crucify!' is all their breath,
And for his death they thirst and cry.

Why, what hath my Lord done?
What makes this rage and spite?
He made the lame to run,
He gave the blind their sight.
Sweet injuries! Yet they at these
Themselves displease, and 'gainst him rise.

Here might I stay and sing,
No story so divine;
Never was love, dear King,
Never was grief like thine.
This is my friend, in whose sweet praise
I all my days could gladly spend.

5. Stabat Mater

13th-cent. Latin hymn, trans. Edward Caswall (1814–78)

Stabat Mater dolorosa
Juxta crucem lacrimosa
Dum pendebat Filius.
Stabat Mater lacrimosa.

At the Cross her station keeping,
stood the mournful Mother weeping,
close to her Son to the last.

O quam tristis et afflicta
Fuit illa benedicta
Mater Unigeniti.
Stabat Mater lacrimosa.

O how sad and sore distressed
was that Mother, highly blest,
of the sole-begotten One.

Quis non posset contristari
Christi Matrem contemplari
Dolentem cum Filio?
Stabat Mater lacrimosa.

Can the human heart refrain
from partaking in her pain,
in that Mother's pain untold?

6. The Seven Last Words from the Cross

Will Todd, quoting The Holy Bible

Before the thunder clap, before the sky went black,
Before the temple curtain was rent in two,
Before he breathed his last, before he bowed his head,
Listen to the words that my saviour said.

Before he gave his life, he spoke these words,
Spoke Seven Last Words from the cross.

And as he hung in shame between the worst of men,
As he felt the pain and felt the agony;
Before the earth heaved up and the moon went red,
Listen to the words that my saviour said.

Before he gave his life, he spoke these words,
Spoke Seven Last Words from the cross:

'Father, forgive them, for they know not what they do.'
'Today you will be with me in paradise.'

And as he hung there, he saw his mother's face,
Looked in her eyes and saw the love and grace.
A disciple stood at her side.
Listen to the words that my saviour cried:

'Behold your son, behold your mother.'
That's what he cried from the cross.

He cried in agony, O how he cried to me,
He cried aloud as he hung on the tree.
He was bent in pain and he was close to dead.
Listen to the words that my saviour said:

'My God, why have you forsaken me on the cross?'
He said: 'I thirst.'
'It is finished.'
'Into your hands, Father, I commit my spirit.'
That's how he died on the cross.

Hear the precious words that my saviour said,
Before the sky went black.

7. My Love has Died for Me

Will Todd

My Lord is gone away,
My Lord is gone away,
My Lord is gone away and I have no place to go.

My friend is lost to me,
My friend is lost to me,
My friend is lost to me and I have no place to go.

The fire that leapt so brightly
Burned into eternity,
Heaven taken from me.

My love has died for me,
My love has died for me,
My love has died for me. I have no place to go.

8. Do not stand at my grave and weep

Mary Elizabeth Frye (1905–2004)

Do not stand at my grave and weep;
I am not there. I do not sleep.

I am a thousand winds that blow.
I am the diamond glints on snow.
I am the sunlight on ripened grain.
I am the gentle autumn rain.

When you awaken in the morning's hush,
I am the swift uplifting rush
Of quiet birds in circled flight.
I am the soft stars that shine at night.

Do not stand at my grave and cry;
I am not there. I did not die.
Do not stand at my grave and weep.

9. Were you there?

American Spiritual text

Were you there when they crucified my Lord?
Sometimes it causes me to tremble, tremble;
Were you there when they crucified my Lord?

Were you there when they laid him in the tomb?
Sometimes it causes me to tremble, tremble;
Were you there when they laid him in the tomb?

Were you there when they nailed him to the tree?
Sometimes it causes me to tremble, tremble;
Were you there when they nailed him to the tree?

Were you there when he rose out of the tomb?

We believe it was for us he rose from the dead.
He died for us and he rose for us.
He died to save us.

(reprise from Movement 1)

Greater love has no man than this, no greater love than this, than to lay down his life for his friends.
There is no greater love than this.

Also available:

Passion Music score and set of parts (pno, bass, drum kit, sax (sop/alto), tpt, tbn, timp/perc)
(ISBN 978-0-19-352565-8)

A complete backing track and individual rehearsal tracks for the vocal parts are also available to download from www.oup.com/passionmusic.

Passion Music

Commissioned for the choirs of St Martin-in-the-Fields, London

Passion Music

WILL TODD

1. *Greater Love*

John 15: 13

© Oxford University Press 2018

Printed in Great Britain

OXFORD UNIVERSITY PRESS, MUSIC DEPARTMENT, GREAT CLARENDON STREET, OXFORD OX2 6DP

The Moral Rights of the Composer have been asserted. Photocopying this copyright material is ILLEGAL.

23
S./A.
SOPRANOS & ALTOS unis.
mp
Great - er love has no
29
man, no great - er love than this,
B♭13
Cm11
34
mf
than to lay down his
E♭/F F/G Cm11
E♭/F F/G Cm11
39
life for his friends.
D7(♯9)
E♭/F F/G

45
Great-er love has no man than this.
Cm11
Bb13
F/G
Cm11
Eb/F F/G
51
mf
Great-er love, great-er, great-er love,
mf
Great-er love, great-er love, great-er love,
TENORS & BASSES unis. mf
Great-er love has no man, no great-er
Cm11
Eb/F F/G Cm11
Eb/F F/G Cm11
mp
57
no great-er, no great-er love than this, to lay down
great-er love, no great-er love than to lay down his
T.
love than this, than to lay down his
B.
Bb13
Cm11
Eb/F F/G Cm11

63
for his friends.
life for his friends.
life for his friends.
D7(♯9)
mf
68
f
Great - er love, great - er love has no man than this.
Great - er love, great - er love has no man than this.
Great - er love, great - er love has no man than this.
E♭/F F/G Cm11
F(sus4)
F/G
f

73
ff
There is no great - er love than
ff
There is no great - er love than
ff
There is no great - er love than
Cm11
E♭/F F/G
Cm11
B♭13
A7(♯9)
D7(♯9)
A♭13
F/G
79
GOSPEL SOLOIST
f
Great - - - - ter love,
3
S.
this.
A.
this.
T.
B.
this.
Cm11
E♭/F F/G
Cm11
E♭/F

84
great - - - - - - er love,
f
Great - er love,
great - er love,
Great - er love,
great - er love,
Great - er love,
great - er love,
89
no great - er love,
great - er love has no man.
great - er love has no man.
great - er love has no man.
D7/F♯
Gm9
A♭maj13
sub. p
Ped.

95
mf
no love is great - er,
p
p
p
F/G
Cm11
mf
p
100
mp
no great - - - er love
3
3
mp
No great - - er love,
mp
No great - - er love,
unis. mp
No great - - er love,
cresc.

105
f
there is no great - er love than this, there is no
there is no great - er love than this, there is no
there is no great - er love than this, there is no
B♭13 A7(♯9) D7(♯9) A♭13 F/G Cm11 B♭13
110
than this, than this.
great - er love than this.
great - er love than this.
great - er love than this.
A7(♯9) D7(♯9) A♭13 F/G

115
Great - er love has no man, no great - er
Great - er love, great - er love has no man,
Great - er love has no man, no great - er
unis.
Great - er love has no man, no great - er
F♯/G♯
C♯m11
120
love than this, than to
no great - er love than this,
love than this, than to
love than this,
T.
B.
than to
B13
C♯m11
E/A♯
D♯m/B
C♯m/C

124
lay down his life for his friends.
than to lay down his life for his friends.
div.
lay down his life for his friends.
lay down his life for his friends.
C♯m11
E♭7(♯9)
129
Great - er love,
unis.
Great - er love, great - er
Great - er love, great - er
Great - er love, great - er
E/F♯
F♯/G♯
Amaj7/B
G13(♯11)

134
mf
cresc.
great - er love has no man,
fp
love has no man than this.
fp
love has no man than this.
fp
love has no man than this.
E/F♯
F♯/G♯
fp
139
ff
no great - er love than this,
ff
div.
love than this,
There is no great - er love than this, there is no great - er
ff
There is no great - er love than this, there is no great - er
ff
There is no great - er love than this, there is no great - er
B13
B♭7(♯9)
E♭7(♯9)
A13
F♯/G♯
C♯m11
B13
B♭7(♯9)
E♭7(♯9)
ff

145
no great - er love than this,
love than this,
love than this, there is no great - er love.
love than this, there is no great - er love.
love than this, there is no great - er love.
A13 F♯/G♯ C♯m11 B13 B♭7(♯9) E♭7(♯9) A13 F♯/G♯
150
colla voce
no great-er love than this.
colla voce

2. *We Believe*

Mrs Cecil Frances Alexander (1818–95)

© Oxford University Press 2018. Photocopying this copyright material is ILLEGAL.

12
save us all.
We may not know, we can - not
D/E
E
D/E
E
G13(♯11)
F♯m11
A/B
15
tell, what pains he had to bear,
rit.
p
E(add2)/G♯
D7
C♯m9
C7(♯11)
A♭7(♭9)
A(♯4)
8vb
18
In time ♩. = 72
p
but we be - lieve,
S./A.
T./B.
p unis.
cresc. poco a poco
We be - lieve, we be -
unis.
p
cresc. poco a poco
In time ♩. = 72
E♭(sus4)
D♭/E♭
A♭/E♭
E♭(sus4)
D♭/E♭
A♭/E♭
E♭(sus4)
pp
cresc. poco a poco
(8)

21
ad lib.
cresc. poco a poco
we be-lieve, we be - lieve
-lieve, we be - lieve, we be - lieve, we
D♭/E♭ A♭/E♭ E♭(sus4) D♭/E♭ G♭/A♭ A♭/B♭ E♭(sus4) D♭/E♭ A♭/E♭ E♭(sus4)
24
ad lib. (E♭ minor pentatonic)
S.
A.
T.
B.
f
be - lieve, we be-lieve, we be-lieve
D♭/E♭ A♭/E♭ E♭(sus4) D♭/E♭

(GOSPEL SOLOIST)
27
più f
it was for us, it was for us, it was for us,
S.
it was for us, it was for us, it was for us,
A.
it was for us, it was for us, it was for us,
T.
it was for us, it was for us, it was for us,
B.
it was for us, it was for us, it was for us,
E♭(sus4) D♭/E♭ A♭/E♭ D♭13 C7(♯9) F7(♯9) A♭/B♭ E♭(sus4) D♭/E♭ A♭/E♭ D♭13
30
ff
it was for us, it was for us, for us,
it was for us, it was for us, for us,
it was for us, it was for us, it was for us,
it was for us, it was for us, it was for us,
it was for us, it was for us, it was for us,
C7(♯9) F7(♯9) A♭/B♭ E♭m(add4) A♭13 D♭13 C7(♯9) F7(♯9) A♭/B♭

33
dim.
it was for us, for us, for us
it was for us, for us, for us.
it was for us, for us, for us
it was for us, for us, for us
it was for us, for us, for us
E♭m(add4)
A♭13
D♭13
C7(♯9)
F7(♯9)
A♭/B♭
E♭(sus4)
D♭/E♭
36
♩. = ♩
p espress.
rit.
he hung, he hung and suf - fered there.
he hung and suf - fered there.
he hung and suf - fered there.
he hung and suf - fered there.
A♭m9
B♭7(♯9)
E♭m6
C♭maj7
pp
Ped.

41
Slower ♩ = 52
pp
mp
He died that we might be for - giv'n, died to make us
He died that we might be for - giv - en, he died to make us
He died that we might be for - giv - en, he died to make us
He died, he died to make us
Slower ♩ = 52
B♭5
C♭maj7/B♭
B♭5
C♭maj7/B♭
A♭m11
8vb
44
good, that we might go at last to hea - ven, saved by his
good, that we might go to hea - - ven, by his
good, that we might go to hea - - ven, by his
good, that we might go to hea - - ven, by his
E♭(add2)/G
E♭m9/G♭
C♭maj13(♯11)
F7(♯9)

47
rit.
colla voce
mp
cresc.
There was no o - ther, no o - ther
mf
pre-cious blood, his pre-cious blood.
pre-cious blood, his pre-cious blood.
pre-cious blood, his pre-cious blood.
pre-cious blood, his pre-cious blood.
E♭m11
C♭maj13
E♭m/F
D7(♯9)
Gm11
B♭/C
mp
50
rit.
p
good e - nough to pay the price of sin;
F(add2)/A
E♭7
Dm9
D♭13(♯11)
A7(♭9)
B♭(♯4)
3
8vb

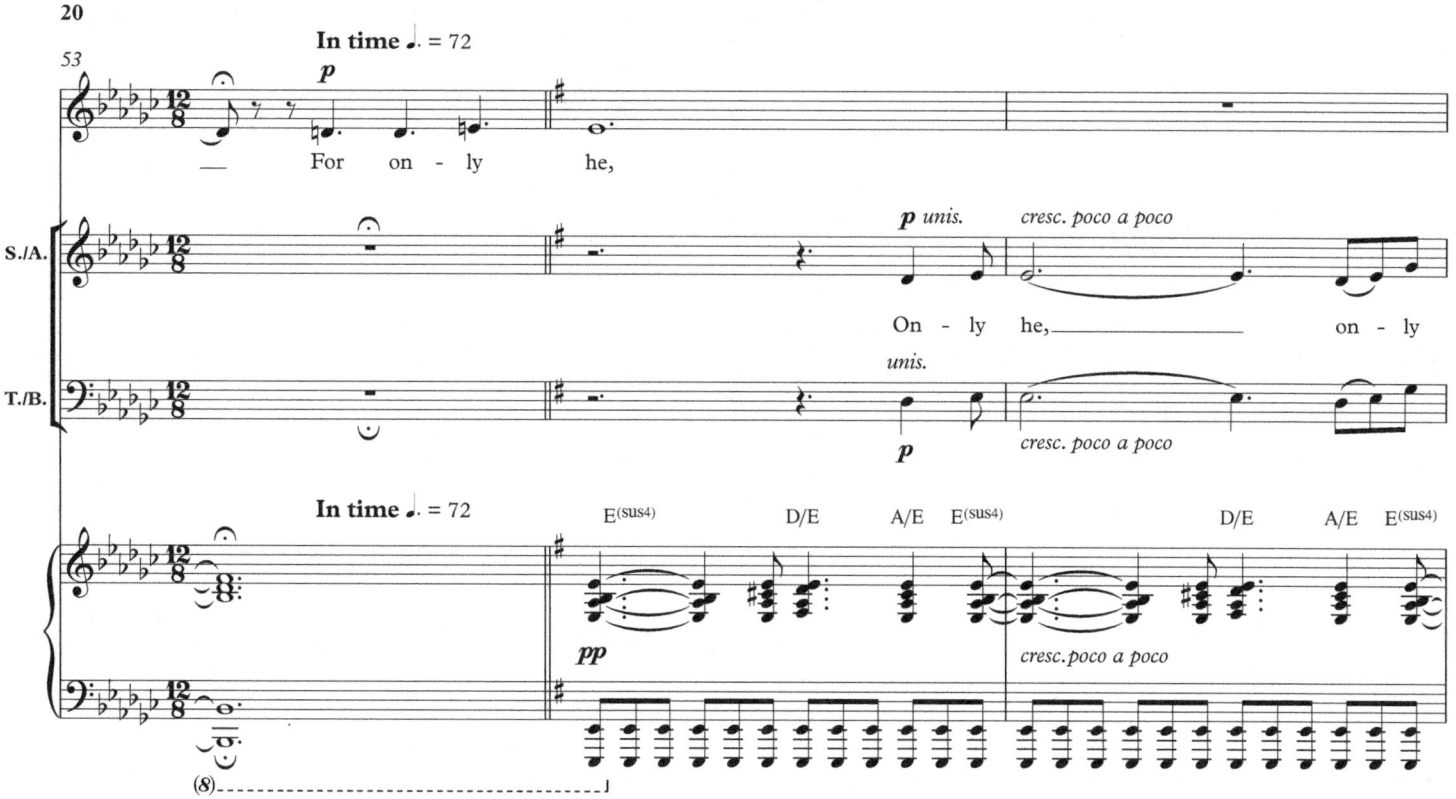
53
In time ♩. = 72
p
For on - ly he,
S./A.
p unis.
cresc. poco a poco
On - ly he, on - ly
T./B.
unis.
p
cresc. poco a poco
In time ♩. = 72
E(sus4) D/E A/E E(sus4) D/E A/E E(sus4)
pp
cresc. poco a poco
(8)

56
ad lib.
on - ly he could un-lock the gate,
he, on - ly he could un - lock the gate, the gate of
D/E A/E E(sus4) D/E G/A A/B E(sus4) D/E A/E E(sus4)

59
ad lib. (E♭ minor pentatonic)
S.
A.
T.
B.
f
hea - ven.
and
let us in,
let us in,
D/E
A/E
E(sus4)
D/E
f
(GOSPEL SOLOIST)
62
più f
the gate of hea - ven,
the gate of hea - ven,
the gate of hea - ven.
S.
A.
T.
B.
E(sus4)
D/E
A/E
D13
C♯7(♯9)
F♯7(♯9)
A/B
E(sus4)
D/E
A/E
D13

65
ff
He died for us, for us,
the gate of hea - ven.
He died for us, for us,
the gate of hea - ven.
He died for us, he died for us,
the gate of hea - ven.
He died for us, he died for us,
the gate of hea - ven.
He died for us, he died for us,
C#7(#9) F#7(#9) A/B Em(add4) A13 D13 C#7(#9) F#7(#9) A/B
68
he died for us, for us,
he died for us, for us,
he died for us, he died for us,
he died for us, he died for us,
he died for us, he died for us,
Em(add4) A13 D13 C#7(#9) F#7(#9) A/B

70
mf
cresc.
he died for us, for us, for us,
sub. p
he died for us, for us, for us,
he died for us, for us, for us,
he died for us, for us, for us,
he died for us, for us, for us,
Em(add4)
G/A
73
ff
rit.
for us.
A/B
E(sus4)
sff

3. *A New Commandment*

John 13: 34

© Oxford University Press 2018. Photocopying this copyright material is ILLEGAL.

16
mf unis.
new com-mand - ment:
That you love,
mf unis.
That you love,
Gm9
Ab m9
Bb m9
mf
con Ped.
21
you love,
love one a - no - ther
you love,
love,
love as
Gm9
Ab m9
Bb m9
Bm9
Em9
f
3
25
as I have loved
you.
f
3
I have loved
you.
Bm9
Em9
C#7(#9)
F#m9
Gm9
Am9
f

29
Love one a - no - - - - ther,
F♯m9
Gm9
Am9
B♭m9
E♭m9
33
love one a - no-ther, love one a - no - ther,
B♭m9
E♭m9
C7(♯9)
D♭(add2)/F
E♭/F
37
unis.
love one a - no-ther, love one a - no - ther, love one a - no-ther, love one a - no - ther,
unis.
D♭(add2)/F
E♭/F
D♭(add2)/F
E♭/F

41
ff
love one a - no - ther.
I give you a new com-mand - ment,
G(sus4)
f
p
f
ff
ff
Ped.
45
I give you a new com-mand - ment: love one a - no - ther,
Dm11
mp
G♭maj9/A♭
49
love one a - no - ther as I have loved you.
Em11
f
A♭maj9/B♭
G(sus4)
ff

53
p unis.
Love one a - no - ther,
love one a - no - ther,
C7(♯9)
Bb7(♯9)
p
57
love one a - no - ther,
love one a - no - ther,
C7(♯9)
Bb7(♯9)
61
love one a - no - ther,
love one a - no - ther,
unis.
Love one a - no - ther,
love one a - no - ther,
C7(♯9)
Bb7(♯9)

65
love one a - no - ther,
love one a - no - ther,
love one a - no - ther,
love one a - no - ther,
C7(♯9)
B♭7(♯9)
69
mf
love,
love,
mf
love one a - no - ther,
love one a - no - ther,
mf
love one a - no - ther,
love one a - no - ther,
B/C♯
A/B
mf
73
love,
love,
love one a - no - ther,
love one a - no - ther,
love one a - no - ther,
love one a - no - ther,
B/C♯
A/B

77
f
love,
love,
f
love one a - no - ther,
love one a - no - ther,
f
T.
B.
love one a - no - ther,
love one a - no - ther,
F/G
E♭/F
f

81
love,
love,
love one a - no - ther,
love one a - no - ther,
love one a - no - ther,
love one a - no - ther,
F/G
E♭/F

85
ff
love one a - no - ther, love one a - no - ther as
ff div.
love one a - no - ther, love one a - no - ther as
ff
love one a - no - ther, love one a - no - ther as
Dm11
G♭maj9/A♭
Em11
A♭maj9/B♭
ff
89
p
I have loved you, as I have loved you,
unis.
p
I have loved you, as I have loved you,
p
I have loved you, as I have loved you,
G(sus4)
Fm9
F♯m9
G♯m9
p
con Ped.

93
S.
A.
T.
B.
Fm9
F♯m9
G♯m9
Am9
Dm9
97
mp unis.
as I have loved you.
unis.
mp
Am9
Dm9
B7(♯9)
Em9
Fm9
Gm9
mp
101
mf
mf
That you love,
that you love,
mf
mf
Em9
Fm9
Gm9
A♭m9
D♭m9

105
mf
that you love,
that you love,
that you love,
that you love,
A♭m9
D♭m9
D7(♯9)
Gm9
A♭m9
B♭m9
109
you love,
love one a - no - ther
you love,
love,
love as
Gm9
A♭m9
B♭m9
Bm9
Em9
113
f
as I have loved
you.
I have loved
you.
Bm9
Em9
C♯7(♯9)
F♯m9
Gm9
Am9

117
Love one a - no - - - - ther,
F♯m9
Gm9
Am9
B♭m9
E♭m9
121
love one a - no-ther, love one a - no - ther,
B♭m9
E♭m9
C7(♯9)
D♭(add2)/F
E♭/F
f
125
unis.
love one a - no-ther, love one a - no - ther.
love one a - no-ther, love one a - no - ther,
unis.
D♭(add2)/F
E♭/F
D♭(add2)/F
E♭/F

129
S.
A.
T.
B.
love one a - no - ther, love one a - no - ther, love one a - no - ther, love one a - no - ther,
love one a - no - ther, love one a - no - ther, love one a - no - ther, love one a -
love one a - no - ther, love one a - no - ther, love one a - no - ther, love one a - no - ther.
love one a - no - ther, love one a - no - ther, love one a - no - ther, love one a -
D♭(add2)/F
E♭/F
E(add2)/G♯
F♯/G♯
f p
mf
f
133
love one a - no - ther, love one a - no - ther, love one a - no - ther, love one a - no - ther,
-no - ther, love one a - no - ther,
love one a - no - ther, love one a - no - ther, love one a - no - ther, love one a - no - ther,
-no - ther, love one a - no - ther,
E(add2)/G♯
F♯/G♯
E(add2)/G♯
F♯/G♯

137
love one a - no - ther, love one a - no - ther, love one a - no - ther!
E(add2)/G♯
F♯/G♯
f p
mf
f
Ped.
141
ff
I give you a new com - mand - ment,

145
I give you a new com - mand - ment, I give you a new com - mand - ment:
I give you a new com-mand - ment, I give you a new com-mand - ment:
I give you a new com-mand - ment, I give you a new com-mand - ment:
I give you a new com-mand - ment, I give you a new com-mand - ment:
Dm9
149
fff
love, love, love one a - no - ther.
Bb13(♯11)
C5
8vb

4. *Love Unknown*

Samuel Crossman (1624–84)

© Oxford University Press 2018. Photocopying this copyright material is ILLEGAL.

11
that they might love - ly be.
O who am I,
that for my
Cm9
F7(sus4)
Fm9(b5)
Fm9(b5)/Bb
Eb(add2)
Ebmaj9/G
14
sake
my Lord should take frail flesh
and die,
and
Ab(add2)
Ab(add2)/G
Db7(#11)
Ab/Bb
Am(b5)
Ab
17
(GOSPEL SOLOIST)
In time (♩ = 52)
die?
S.
mp
He came from
A.
p
He came from
T.
B.
In time (♩ = 52)
Db13
C7(#9)
Cbmaj7
Fm7/Bb

19
his blest throne, sal - va - tion to bes-tow;
mp
his throne, sal - - va - tion to bes-tow; but men made
p
mp
He came from his blest throne, sal - va - tion to bes-tow; but men made
p
mp
He came from his blest throne, sal - - va - tion to bes-tow; but men made
Fm11
G7(♯9)
A♭maj9
Fm11
C♭9
p
3
22
but men made strange, and none the longed-for Christ would know. But O, my
strange, and none, none the Christ would know. O,
strange, and none, none the Christ would know.
strange, and none Christ would know. But
B♭7(sus4)
D♭9
Cm9
F7(sus4)
Fm9(♭5)
Fm9(♭5)/B♭
3

25
mf
friend, my friend in - deed, who at my need his life did
mf
my friend in - deed, who at my need his life did
mf
My friend in - deed, who at my need his life did
mf
O, my friend in - deed, who at my need his life did
E♭(add2)
E♭maj9/G
A♭(add2)
A♭(add2)/G
Fm11
Fm7/B♭
mp
28
GOSPEL SOLOIST
mf
Some - times they strew his way and his sweet
S.
(mf)
spend. Some - times they strew his way and his sweet
A.
(mf)
spend. Some - times they strew his way and his sweet
T.
mp
spend. ah
B.
mp
spend. ah
E♭(add2)
A♭(add2)
G♭+7
F7(sus4)
Fm7/B♭
mf
3

31
prai - ses sing; re - sound-ing all the day ho - san - nas to their
prai - ses sing; re - sound-ing all the day ho - san - nas to their
prai - ses sing; re - sound-ing all the day ho - san - nas to their
His prai - ses sing, all the day ho - san - nas to their
His prai - ses sing, all the day ho - san - nas to their
E♭(add2)
D♭+7
Cm9
F(sus4)
F13(♯11)
Em11
G/A
34
King. Then 'cru - ci - fy!' is all their breath, and for his
King. Then 'cru - ci - fy!' is all their breath, and for his
King. Then 'cru - ci - fy!' is all their breath, and for his
King. Then 'cru - ci - fy!' is all their breath, and for his
King. Then 'cru - ci - fy!' is all their breath, and for his
D(add2)
Dmaj7
F♯(sus4)
F♯(♯5)/E
E♭7(sus4)
E♭7
F♭maj7

37
p
death they thirst and cry.
death they thirst and cry.
death they thirst and cry.
death they thirst and cry.
death they thirst and cry.
A♭m11
Fm7(♭5)
Fm7(♭5)/B♭
G7(♯5)
A♭maj7
40
D♭13
C7(♯9)
C♭maj7
A♭/B♭
G7/B
Cm11
mf
43
GOSPEL SOLOIST
mf
Why, what hath my Lord done?
A♭(♯4)
Fm11
3

45
What has he done to make this rage and spite?
G7(♯9)
A♭maj9
Fm11
C♭9
47
(GOSPEL SOLOIST)
He made the lame to run, he gave the blind their sight. Sweet in - ju -
S.
A.
T.
B.
p (stagger breathing)
ah
B♭7(sus4)
D♭9
Cm9
F7(sus4)
Fm9(♭5)
Fm9(♭5)/B♭

50
-ries! Yet they at these them-selves dis - please, and 'gainst him
(ah)
(ah)
(ah)
E♭(add2)
E♭maj9/G
A♭(add2)
A♭(add2)/G
D♭7(♯11)
A♭/B♭
53
rit.
rise,
rise.
mp
f
Rise.
Here might I
(ah)
(ah)
(ah)
(ah)
Am(♭5)
A♭
D♭13
C7(♯9)
C♭maj7
Fm7/B♭

56
a tempo
stay and sing, here might I stay and sing, no sto - ry so di -
stay and sing, no sto - ry so di-vine;
stay and sing, no sto - ry so di-vine;
stay and sing, no sto - ry so di-vine;
a tempo
Fm11
G7(♯9)
A♭maj9
Fm11
C♭9
f
59
f
Ne - ver was love, dear King, ne - ver was grief like thine. This is my
-vine; ne - ver was love, dear King, ne - ver grief like thine.
ne - ver was love, dear King, ne - ver was grief like thine. This is my
ne - ver was love, dear King, ne - ver was grief, ne - ver grief like thine. My
ne - ver was love, dear King, ne - ver was grief like thine. This is my
B♭7(sus4)
D♭9
Cm9
F7(sus4)
Fm9(♭5)
Fm9(♭5)/B♭

62
rit.
a tempo
friend.
ff
My friend, in whose sweet praise,
ff
friend, this is my friend, in whose sweet praise I all my
ff
friend, this is my friend, in whose sweet praise I all my
ff
friend, this is my friend, in whose sweet praise I all my
rit.
a tempo
E♭(add2)
E♭maj9/G
G♭13(♯11)
F(add2)
Fmaj9/A
B♭(add2)
B♭(add2)/A
ff
65
p
mf
p
this is my friend, in whose sweet
days could glad - - ly spend, friend, in whose sweet
mf
p
days could glad - - ly spend, friend, in whose sweet
mf
p
days could glad - - ly spend, friend,
E♭7(♯11)
B♭/C
Bm(♭5)
B♭
F(add2)
Fmaj9/A
mf
p

68
p
I all my days could glad - - - ly spend,
pp
praise
mp
could glad - ly
pp
praise.
pp
praise.
pp
praise.
B♭(add2)
B♭(add2)/A
E♭7(♯11)
B♭/C
Bm(♭5)
B♭
71
(GOSPEL SOLOIST)
rit.
a tempo
spend all my days,
S.
spend.
rit.
a tempo
E♭13
D7(♯9)
D♭maj7
Gm7/C
A7(♯5)
B♭maj7
74
(GOSPEL SOLOIST)
rit.
spend all my days.
B♭/C
A7/C♯
Dm11
B♭(♯4)
F

to inspirational mothers Mary, Jean, and Iris

5. *Stabat Mater*

13th-cent. Latin hymn

© Oxford University Press 2018. Photocopying this copyright material is ILLEGAL.

7
(in time)
p
pp
-us.
Sta - - bat
(in time)
Dm11
Gm11
Ped.
10
mp
mf
Ma - - ter la - - cri - - mo - - sa,
Dm11
Gm11
C(sus4)

13
mp
pp
la - - cri - - mo - - sa.
Gm11
A7(♯9 ♭9)
(tempo can ebb and flow)
16
p
O quam tri - stis et af - fli - cta fu - it il - la be - ne -
(tempo can ebb and flow)

19
mf
- di - cta Ma - ter U - ni - - ge - ni - -
mf
- di - cta Ma - ter U - ni - - ge - ni - -
mf
- di - cta U - ni - - ge - ni - -
mf
- di - cta U - ni - - ge - ni - -
(in time)
22
p pp p
-ti. Sta - - bat
p pp p
-ti. Sta - - bat
p pp p
-ti. Sta - - bat
p pp p
-ti. Sta - - bat
(in time)
Dm11
Gm11
pp
p
Ped.

25
mp
p
mf
Ma - - ter la - - cri - - mo - - sa,
Ma - - ter la - - cri - - mo - - sa,
Ma - - ter la - - cri - - mo - - sa,
Ma - - ter la - - cri - - mo - - sa,
Dm11
Gm11
C(sus4)
28
pp
la - - cri - - mo - - sa.
la - - cri - - mo - - sa.
la - - cri - - mo - - sa.
la - - cri - - mo - - sa.
Gm11
A7(♯9/♭9)

(tempo can ebb and flow)
31
p
Quis non pos - set con - tri - sta - ri, Chri - sti Ma - trem con - tem -
Quis non pos - set con - tri - sta - ri, Chri - sti Ma - trem con - tem -
Quis non pos - set con - tri - sta - ri, Chri - sti Ma - trem con - tem -
Quis non pos - set con - tri - sta - ri, Chri - sti Ma - trem con - tem -
(tempo can ebb and flow)
34
mf
-pla - ri do - len - tem cum Fi - li - -
- pla - ri do - len - tem cum Fi - li - -
-pla - ri -len - tem cum Fi - li - -
-pla - ri -len - tem cum Fi - li - -

(in time)
37
SOPRANO SOLO (or SEMI-CHORUS)
p espress.
mf
Sta - bat Ma - ter
S.
A.
T.
B.
-o?
Sta - bat Ma - ter
(in time)
Dm11
Gm11
Dm11
pp
p
mp
Ped.
41
la - - - cri - mo - sa,
la - cri -
la - - cri - - mo - - sa, la - - cri - -
Gm11
C(sus4)
Gm11
mf
mp

44
p
-mo - - - - - - sa.
pp
-mo - - sa, la - - cri - -
pp
-mo - - sa, la - - cri - -
pp
-mo - - sa, la - - cri - -
pp
-mo - - sa, la - - cri - -
A7(♯9/♭9)
Gm11
p
rit.
47
ppp
S.
-mo - - sa.
ppp
A.
-mo - - sa.
ppp
T.
-mo - - sa.
ppp
B.
-mo - - sa.
rit.
A7(♯9/♭9)
Gm11
Dm9 (maj7)
pp
ppp
8va
8vb

6. *The Seven Last Words from the Cross*

Will Todd, quoting The Holy Bible

© Oxford University Press 2018. Photocopying this copyright material is ILLEGAL.

17
Se-ven Last Words from the cross,
Se-ven Last Words,
C#5 Amaj7/C# Gmaj7/C# G#7(#5) C#5 Amaj7/C# A13(#11) G#7(#5) C#5 Amaj7/C# Gmaj7/C# G#7(#5)
8vb
20
Se-ven Last Words, Se-ven Last Words from the cross.
C#5 Amaj7/C# Gmaj7/C# G#7(#5) C#5 Amaj7/C# A13(#11) G#7(#5) C#(sus4)/G#
8va
8vb
Ped.
GOSPEL SOLOIST
23
f
And as he hung in shame be-tween the worst of men, as he
S./A.
T./B.
(8)
mf

26
(GOSPEL SOLOIST)
felt the pain and felt the a - go - ny; be - fore the earth heaved up and the
29
(GOSPEL SOLOIST)
moon went red, lis - ten to the words that my sa - viour said. Be - fore he
S. A.
f
Lis - ten to the words that my sa - viour said. Be - fore he
T. B.
f
f
32
cresc.
gave his life, he spoke these words, spoke
ff
cresc.
gave his life, he spoke these words, spoke
ff
cresc.
ff
D♯5
G♯7(♭9)
mp
cresc.

36
Se-ven Last_ Words, Se-ven Last_ Words from the
unis.
Se-ven Last_ Words, Se-ven Last_ Words, Se-ven Last_ Words from the
C♯5 Amaj7/C♯ Gmaj7/C♯ G♯7(♯5) C♯5 Amaj7/C♯ Gmaj7/C♯ G♯7(♯5) C♯5 Amaj7/C♯ Gmaj7/C♯ G♯7(♯5)
ff

39
cross, Se-ven Last_ Words.
cross, Se-ven Last_ Words, Se-ven Last_ Words,
C♯5 Amaj7/C♯ A13(♯11) G♯7(♯5) C♯5 Amaj7/C♯ Gmaj7/C♯ G♯7(♯5) C♯5 Amaj7/C♯ Gmaj7/C♯ G♯7(♯5)
8vb

42
S.
A.
Se-ven Last Words from the cross:
T.
B.
p
C♯5
Amaj7/C♯
A13(♯11)
G♯7(♯5)
C♯(sus4)
C♯m11
8vb
Ped.
46
SOPRANOS & ALTOS unis.
mp espress.
'Fa - ther, for - give them, for they know not what they
Dmaj7(♯4)
3
51
do.
Fmaj7(♯4)
A7(♯11)
mp

55
mp
S.
Fa - ther, for - give them, for they know not what they
mp
A.
Fa - ther, for - give them what they
G♯m11
Em7
p
59
p
S.
do.'
p
A.
do.'
TENORS & BASSES unis.
mf
T./B.
'To-
B/C♯
mf
E13
63
T./B.
- day you will be with me in pa - ra - dise.
G♭(add2)
A♭/B♭
B♭7(♯5)
E♭m(maj7)
p
mf
Ped.

68
To - day
G13(♯11)
F♯m11
Ped.
73
p
rit.
you will be with me in pa - ra - dise.'
Dm(maj7)
B♭maj7
A7(♯9)
Dm9
pp
Dramatic and very free—colla voce
GOSPEL SOLOIST
78
And as he hung there, he saw his mo-ther's face, looked in her eyes and saw the
Gm/A
ad lib.
8vb
82
In time ♩ = 144
love and grace. A dis - ci - ple stood at her side. Lis - ten to the words that my
(8)

86
(GOSPEL SOLOIST)
sa - viour cried:
S.
A.
f
cresc.
'Be - hold your son, be - hold your
T.
B.
f
cresc.
E5
A7(b9)
f cresc.
90
ff
mo - ther.' That's what he cried, that's what he cried, that's what he cried from the
ff
D5
B♭maj7/D
B♭13(♯11)
A7(b9/♯5)
D5
B♭maj7/D
B♭13(♯11)
A7(b9/♯5)
D5
B♭maj7/D
B♭13(♯11)
A7(b9/♯5)
ff

94
That's what he cried, that's what he cried,
cross.
That's what he cried, that's what he cried,
D5 B♭maj7/D B♭13(♯11) A7(♭9/♯5) D5 B♭maj7/D B♭13(♯11) A7(♭9/♯5) D5 B♭maj7/D B♭13(♯11) A7(♭9/♯5)
8vb
97
that's what he cried from the cross.
He cried in
f
that's what he cried from the cross.
He cried in
f unis.
unis.
f
D5 B♭maj7/D B♭13(♯11) A7(♭9/♯5) B♭7 B♭7(sus4)
8va
8vb

100
a - go - ny, O how he cried to me, he cried a - loud as he hung on the tree. He was
a - go - ny, O how he cried to me, he cried a - loud as he hung on the tree. He was
E♭m
f
(8)
104
bent in pain and he was close to dead. Lis-ten to the words that my sa - viour said:
bent in pain and he was close to dead. Lis-ten to the words that my sa - viour said: 'My
(8)

108
cresc.
God, why have you, why have you
cresc.
F5
Bb7(b9)
sub. p
cresc.
112
ff
for - sa - ken me, for - sa - ken me, for - sa - ken me on the
ff
Eb5 Cbmaj7/Eb Cb13(#11) Bb7(b9 #5)
Eb5 Cbmaj7/Eb Cb13(#11) Bb7(b9 #5)
Eb5 Cbmaj7/Eb Cb13(#11) Bb7(b9 #5)
ff

115
ff
'For - sa - ken me, for - sa - ken me,
cross, for - sa - ken me, for - sa - ken me,
E♭5 C♭maj7/E♭ C♭13(♯11) B♭7(♭9/♯5) E♭5 C♭maj7/E♭ C♭13(♯11) B♭7(♭9/♯5) E♭5 C♭maj7/E♭ C♭13(♯11) B♭7(♭9/♯5)
118
for - sa - ken me on the cross? Why
for - sa - ken me on the cross? Why
E♭5 C♭maj7/E♭ C♭13(♯11) B♭7(♭9/♯5) E♭5 C♭maj7/E♭ C♭13(♯11) B♭7(♭9/♯5) E♭5 C♭maj7/E♭ C♭13(♯11) B♭7(♭9/♯5)

121
dim.
have you for -
dim.
have you for -
dim.
E♭5 C♭maj7/E♭ C♭13(♯11) B♭7(♭9/♯5) E♭5 C♭maj7/E♭ C♭13(♯11) B♭7(♭9/♯5) E♭5 C♭maj7/E♭ C♭13(♯11) B♭7(♭9/♯5)
dim.
124
pp mf
- - - sa - - ken me?' He
pp
- - - sa - - ken me?'
pp
E♭5 C♭maj7/E♭ C♭13(♯11) B♭7(♭9/♯5) E♭5 C♭maj7/E♭ C♭13(♯11) B♭7(♭9/♯5) E♭5 C♭maj7/E♭ C♭13(♯11)
p
8vb

128
(GOSPEL SOLOIST)
said:
S.
p
'I thirst.'
A.
p
'I thirst.'
T.
p
'I thirst.'
B.
p
'I thirst.'
sax (ad lib.)
mp espress.
133
mp
'It is fi - nished,
mp
'It is fi - nished,
mp
'It is fi - nished,
mp
'It is fi - nished,

137
rit.
mf
it is fi - nished.'
mf
it is fi - nished.'
mf
it is fi - nished.'
mf
it is fi - nished.'
rit.
142
Slower ♩ = 104
mp
'In - to your hands, Fa - ther, I com -
rit.
pp
ah
pp
ah
pp
ah
Slower ♩ = 104
rit.
pp

a tempo (♩ = 104)
146
(GOSPEL SOLOIST)
-mit my spi - rit.'
That's how he died on the
E♭5 C♭maj7/E♭ C♭13(♯11) B♭7(♭9/♯5)
149
(GOSPEL SOLOIST)
cross.
S./A.
pp unis.
cresc.
That's how he died, that's how he died,
T./B.
unis.
pp
cresc.
152
accel. poco a poco
ad lib. (E♭ minor pentatonic)
mf
that's how he died on the cross.
That's how he died,
mf
accel. poco a poco
mf

155
cresc.
that's how he died, that's how he died on the cross.
cresc.
E♭5 C♭maj7/E♭ C♭13(♯11) B♭7(♭9 ♯5) E♭5 C♭maj7/E♭ C♭13(♯11) B♭7(♭9 ♯5) E♭5 C♭maj7/E♭ C♭13(♯11) B♭7(♭9 ♯5)
cresc.
158
In time ♩ = 126
f
cresc.
That's how he died, that's how he died, that's how he died on the
f
cresc.
In time ♩ = 126
E♭5 C♭maj7/E♭ C♭13(♯11) B♭7(♭9 ♯5) E♭5 C♭maj7/E♭ C♭13(♯11) B♭7(♭9 ♯5) E♭5 C♭maj7/E♭ C♭13(♯11) B♭7(♭9 ♯5)
f
cresc.

161
ff
cross.
That's how he died, that's how he died,
ff
E♭5 C♭maj7/E♭ C♭13(♯11) B♭7(♭9 ♯5) E♭5 C♭maj7/E♭ C♭13(♯11) B♭7(♭9 ♯5) E♭5 C♭maj7/E♭ C♭13(♯11) B♭7(♭9 ♯5)
ff
rit.
Dramatic and very free
164
f
Hear the pre-cious words that my
that's how he died on the cross.
rit.
Dramatic and very free
E♭5 C♭maj7/E♭ C♭13(♯11) B♭7(♭9 ♯5) B♭7(sus4)

167
rit.
ff
sa - viour said, be - fore the sky went black.
rit.
In time ♩ = 120
molto rit.
170
(GOSPEL SOLOIST)
f
ff
S.
Be - fore the sky went black.
div.
A.
Be - fore the sky went black.
T.
Be - fore the sky went black.
B.
Black.
In time ♩ = 120
molto rit.
sff
Ped.

7. *My Love has Died for Me*

Will Todd

© Oxford University Press 2018. Photocopying this copyright material is ILLEGAL.

20
mp
mf
p
gone a - way and I have no place to go, I have no place to go.
gone a - way and I have no place to go, I have no place to go.
gone a - way and I have no place to go, I have no place to go.
gone a - way and I have no place to go, I have no place to go.
25
pp espress.
My friend is lost to me, my friend is lost to me,
My friend is lost to me, my friend is lost to me, my
My friend is lost to me, my friend is lost to me,
My friend is lost to me, my friend is lost to me,

30
mp
mf
my friend is lost to me and I have no place to go, I have no
friend is lost to me and I have no place to go, I have no
my friend is lost to me and I have no place to go, I have no
my friend is lost to me and I have no place to go, I have no

35
p
f
place to go. The fire that leapt so bright - ly burned in - to e -
place to go. The fire that leapt so bright - ly burned in - to e -
place to go. The fire that leapt so bright - ly burned in - to e -
place to go. The fire that leapt so bright - ly burned in - to e -

40
mp
p
pp espress.
-ter - ni - ty, hea - ven ta - ken from me. My love has
-ter - ni - ty, hea - ven ta - ken from me. My love has
-ter - ni - ty, hea - ven ta - ken from me. My love has
-ter - ni - ty, hea - ven ta - ken from me. My love has
45
died for me, my love has died for me, my love has died for me,
died for me, my love has died for me, my love has died for me,
died for me, my love has died for me, my love has died for me,
died for me, my love has died for me, my love has died for me,

50
mf
f
p
my love has died for me, died for me. I have no
my love has died for me, died for me. I have no
my love has died for me, died for me. I have no
my love has died for me, died for me. I have no
rit.
55
pp
place to go, I have no place to go.
place to go, I have no place to go.
place to go, I have no place to go.
place to go, I have no place to go.
rit.

8. *Do not stand at my grave and weep*

Mary Elizabeth Frye (1905–2004)

© Oxford University Press 2018. Photocopying this copyright material is ILLEGAL.

17
am the dia - mond glints on snow. I am the sun - light on ri - pened grain.
snow. The sun - light on ri - pened grain.
Db maj9/F
Fm11
Bbm11
21
cresc.
I am the gen - tle au - tumn rain.
cresc.
Db (maj9)
C7(#9)
cresc.
24
mp
When you a - wa - ken in the morn - ing's hush,
I am the swift up - lift - ing
mp
Bbm11
Db maj7/Eb
Eb/F
Gm
Gm/F
mp

27
mf
p
rush
of qui - et birds in cir - cled flight.
mf
p
E♭maj9
D♭13(♯11)
Cm9
Cm7/F
B♭(sus4)
B♭(add2)
mf
p
30
I am the soft stars that shine at night.
Do not stand at my
I am stars that shine at night.
A♭(add2)
A♭/E♭
E♭
Fm11
33
molto cresc.
I am not there.
I did not die.
grave and cry;
molto cresc.
I, I did not die.
B♭m11
D♭maj9
B♭m9
molto cresc.

36
ff
molto dim.
I am not there.
ff
molto dim.
C♭/C
B♭m/C
C7(♯9)
ff
mf
39
pp unis. (stagger breathing)
ah
p
mf
Do not stand at my grave and weep, no, do not stand at my grave and
p
senza Ped.
42
(ah)
weep, do not stand at my grave and weep, no,

45
A.
(ah)
mf
do not stand, do not stand at my grave,
do not stand at my grave and weep, do not stand at my grave and
cresc.
mp
48
(ah)
do not stand at my grave and weep, no, do not stand at my grave and
weep, no, do not stand at my grave and weep,
Fm
51
(ah)
weep, no, do not stand at my grave, do not stand at my grave,
do not stand at my grave and weep, no, do not stand at my grave and
B♭m9
Fm
cresc.

54
S.
(ah)
mp
A.
(ah)
Do not stand, do not stand at my grave,
f
T.
do not stand at my grave, do not stand at my grave and
f
B.
weep, do not stand at my grave and weep, no,
f
Fm
mf
57
(ah)
do not stand at my grave and weep, no, do not stand,
weep, no, do not stand at my grave and weep, no,
do not stand at my grave and weep, do not stand at my grave and

60
(ah)
Do not
do not stand at my grave and weep,
do not stand at my grave, do not stand at my grave, do not stand at my grave,
weep, no, do not stand at my grave and weep,
B♭m9
Fm
B♭/C
cresc.
63
stand at my grave and weep, do not stand at my grave, no,
do not stand, do not stand at my grave,
do not stand at my grave and
do not stand at my grave and weep, no,
Fm

65
do not stand at my grave and weep, do not
do not stand at my grave and weep, no,
weep, no, do not stand at my grave and
do not stand at my grave and weep,
67
stand at my grave and weep, do not stand at my grave and weep, do not
do not stand, do not stand at my
weep, no, do not stand at my grave,
do not stand at my grave and weep, no,

69
stand at my grave and weep, do not stand at my grave and weep,
3
grave and weep,
do not stand at my grave, do not stand at my grave,
do not stand at my grave and weep,
71
mf
do not stand at my grave and
mf
do not stand at my grave and weep, no,
mf
do not stand at my grave and weep,
mf
do not stand at my grave and weep, no,
B♭m9
mp

73
p
weep, no, do not stand at my grave and
p
do not stand at my grave and weep,
p
do not stand at my grave and weep,
p
do not stand at my grave and weep,
F(sus4)
p
75
weep,
pp
do not stand at my grave and weep, no,
pp
do not stand at my grave,
pp
do not stand at my grave and weep, no,
B♭m9
pp

77
pp
rit.
do not stand at my grave and weep, no, do not stand at my grave and
do not stand at my grave and weep, do not
do not stand at my grave and weep, do not stand at my grave and
do not stand at my grave and weep, do not
Cm13
rit.
80
mp
Slower
ppp
weep, at my grave. I am not there.
stand at my grave. I am not there.
weep, at my grave. I am not there.
stand at my grave. I am not there.
Db maj9
C7(♯9)
Slower

9. *Were you there?*

American Spiritual text

© Oxford University Press 2018. Photocopying this copyright material is ILLEGAL.

9
p
mf
Lord?
Some - times it cau - ses me to
F♯m11
A/B
B
E
Am9
mf
11
p
trem - ble, trem - ble; were you there when they cru - ci - fied my
D(sus4)
C♯m11
E♭7(sus4)
E♭
Emaj7
p
13
rit.
Lord?
Were you there?
C♯m11
E/F♯
B
Bmaj7/D♯

In time ♩ = 52
15
GOSPEL SOLOIST
mf
Were you there when they laid him in the tomb? Were you
S.
A.
T.
B.
Were you there when they laid him there? Were you
In time ♩ = 52
Fm11
B♭7(sus4)
E♭(sus4)
E♭(add2)/G
A♭(add2)
A♭/B♭ G7/B
18
broadening
there when they laid him in the tomb?
p
mf
Some-times it cau-ses me to
Some - times it cau-ses me to
Some-times it cau-ses me to
Cm9
Fm9
B♭m11
D♭/E♭
E♭

21
p
trem - ble, trem - ble; were you there when they laid him in the tomb? Were you
p
trem - ble, trem - ble; were you there when they laid him in the tomb? Were you
p
trem - ble, trem - ble; were you there when they laid him in the tomb? Were you
p
trem - ble, trem - ble; were you there when they laid him in the tomb? Were you
24
a tempo
f
Were you there when they nailed him to the tree?
mp
Were you
there?
Were you
there?
Were you
there?
Were you
there?
Were you
a tempo
E♭
G7(♯9)
D♭13(♯11)
Cm9
Cm9/B♭
Am7(♭5)
A♭maj7
G7(♯9)
mf
f

27
there? Were you there?
there? Were you there? Some-times it cau-ses me to
there? Were you there? Some-times it cau-ses me to
there? Were you there? Some - times it cau-ses me to
there? Were you there? Some-times it cau-ses me to
Dbm(maj7)
Bbm13(#11)
Am7(b5)
D7(#9)
mp
p
30
Were you
trem - ble, some-times it cau - ses me to trem - ble.
trem - ble, trem - ble, some-times it cau - ses me to trem - ble.
trem - ble, trem - ble, some-times it cau - ses me to trem - ble.
trem - ble, trem - ble, some-times it cau - ses me to trem - ble.
Ebm(maj7)
Bb/C
C
Fm11
Eb(add2)/G
Ab(add2)
Ab/Bb

33
rit.
a tempo
there? Were you there?
pp
Were you there when he rose out of the
Were you there when he rose out of the
Were you there when he rose out of the
Were you there when he rose out of the
A♭m(maj7)
A♭m7/B♭
E♭(sus4)
E♭(add2)/G
36
mf
tomb? Were you there when he rose out of the tomb?
tomb? Were you there when he rose out of, out of the tomb?
tomb? Were you there when he rose out of, out of the tomb?
tomb? Were you there when he rose out of the tomb?
A♭(add2)
G7/B
Cm9
Fm9
B♭m11
D♭/E♭
E♭

39
f
ff
rit.
Were you there? Were you there?
Were you there? Were you there? Were you there?
Were you there? Were you there? Were you there?
Were you there? Were you there? Were you there?
Were you there? Were you there? Were you there?
A♭ B♭/A♭ A♭(add2) E♭/B♭ G7/B Cm Fm9 E♭(add2)/G A♭(sus2)
42
a tempo
Were you there? Were you there when he
Were you there? Were you there? Were you there? Were you
Were you there? Were you there when he rose out of the tomb? Were you
Were you there? Were you there when he rose out of the tomb? Were you
Were you there? Were you there when he rose out of the tomb? Were you
A♭/B♭ E♭(sus4) E♭(add2)/G A♭(add2) G7/B
8vb

45
3
rose out of the tomb? We be - lieve it
there when he rose out of the tomb? We be - lieve it
there when he rose out of the tomb? We be - lieve it
there when he rose out of the tomb? We be - lieve it
there when he rose out of the tomb? We be - lieve it
Cm9 Fm9 Bbm11 Db/Eb Eb Ab Bb/Ab Ab(add2) Eb/Bb G7/B
48
rit.
was for us, for us he rose from the dead.
was for us, for us he rose from the dead.
was for us, for us he rose from the dead.
was for us, for us he rose from the dead.
was for us, for us he rose from the dead.
rit.
Cm Fm9 Eb(add2)/G Ab(sus2) Ab/Bb

Fast swing ♩ = 144
(GOSPEL SOLOIST)
51
S.
A.
T.
B.
f
unis.
We be - lieve it was for us. He
Fast swing ♩ = 144
E♭m
57
died for us, died for us, died for us,
A♭13
F7(♯9)
B13
63
and he rose, he rose for us. He
E♭/F
B♭7(♯9)
E♭m

69
died for us, died for us, and he rose
A♭13
F7(♯9)
B13
75
GOSPEL SOLOIST
ff
f
We, we be -
S. A.
from the dead.
f unis.
We, we be -
T. B.
unis.
ff
f
E♭/F
B♭7(♯9)
E♭m
81
-lieve, we be - lieve,
-lieve, we be - lieve,
A♭13

87
we be lieve it was for us,
we be - lieve it was for us,
F7(♯9)
B13
E♭/F
B♭7(♯9)
Straight ♩. = 72
GOSPEL SOLOIST
93
ff
it was for us, it was for us, it was for us,
S.
it was for us, it was for us, it was for us,
A.
it was for us, it was for us, it was for us,
T.
it was for us, it was for us, it was for us,
B.
it was for us, it was for us, it was for us,
Straight ♩. = 72
E♭(sus4)
D♭/E♭
A♭/E♭
D♭13
C7(♯9)
F7(♯9)
A♭/B♭
E♭(sus4)
D♭/E♭
A♭/E♭
D♭13

96
it was for us. He died for us, for us,
it was for us. He died for us, for us,
it was for us. He died for us, he died for us,
it was for us. He died for us, he died for us,
it was for us. He died for us, he died for us,
C7(♯9) F7(♯9) A♭/B♭ E♭m(add4) A♭13 D♭13 C7(♯9) F7(♯9) A♭/B♭
99
he died for us, for us, he died for us,
he died for us, for us, he died for us,
he died for us, he died for us, he died for us,
he died for us, he died for us, he died for us,
he died for us, he died for us, he died for us,
E♭m(add4) A♭13 D♭13 C7(♯9) F7(♯9) A♭/B♭ E♭m(add4)

102
mf
cresc.
ff
for us, for us, for us,
sub. p
cresc.
for us, for us, for us,
Gb/Ab
Ab/Bb
105
rit.
Freely
he died for us, he
ff
f
for us, he died for us,
Gb13(#11)
F7(#9)
sff
mf
8vb

108
(GOSPEL SOLOIST)
died for us, and rose for
unis.
A.
died for us,
unis.
B.
E♭7(♯9)/B♭ F7(♯9)/B♭ E♭7(♯9)/B♭
(8)
111
cresc.
us, and rose for us,
cresc.
and rose for us, rose for
cresc.
F7(♯9)/B♭ E♭7(♯9)/B♭ F7(♯9)/B♭ E♭7(♯9)/B♭ F7(♯9)/B♭ E♭7(♯9)/B♭ F7(♯9)/B♭ E♭7(♯9)/B♭ F7(♯9)/B♭ E♭7(♯9)/B♭
cresc.
(8)

114
rit.
ff
rose for us. He died to save us.
ff p
us, rose for us.
ff p
rit.
F7(♯9)/B♭ E♭7(♯9)/B♭ sim.
B♭7(♯9)
f p
(8)
118
Slower ♩. = 50
(GOSPEL SOLOIST)
rit.
ad lib.
f ff
S.
He died to save us.
A.
He died to save us.
T.
He died to save us.
B.
He died to save us.
Slower ♩. = 50
rit.
E♭m11
Ped.

Slow, funky ♩ = 76
120
(GOSPEL SOLOIST)
f
Great-er love
Great-er love, great-
Great-er love
TENORS & BASSES unis.
Great-er love
Slow, funky ♩ = 76
drums
E/F♯
F♯/G♯
C♯m11
124
has no man, no great - er love than this,
- er love has no man, no great - er
has no man, no great - er love than this,
has no man, no great - er love than this,
B13

129
than to lay down his life
love than this, than to lay down his life
than to lay down his life
T.
B.
than to lay down his life
C♯m11
E/A♯
D♯m/B
C♯m/C
C♯m11
134
for his friends. Great - er
div.
unis.
for his friends. Great - er
for his friends. Great - er
for his friends. Great - er
E♭7(♯9)
E/F♯
F♯/G♯

139
love, great - er
fp
love, great - er love has no man than this.
fp
love, great - er love has no man than this.
fp
love, great - er love has no man than this.
Amaj7/B
G13(♯11)
E/F♯
F♯/G♯
144
3
love has no man, no great - er
ff
div.
love than this,
There is no great - er love than this,
ff
There is no great - er love than this,
ff
There is no great - er love than this,
B13
B♭7(♯9)
E♭7(♯9)
A13
F♯/G♯
C♯m11

150
love than this, no great-er love than this,
love than this,
there is no great-er love than this, there is no great-er
there is no great-er love than this, there is no great-er
there is no great-er love than this, there is no great-er
B13 Bb7(#9) Eb7(#9) A13 F#/G# C#m11 B13 Bb7(#9) Eb7(#9)
156
colla voce
no great-er love than this.
unis.
love than this.
love than this.
love than this.
A13 F#/G#
colla voce
f
ff